HACIENDA
COURTYARDS

HACIENDA COURTYARDS

Karen Witynski
Joe P. Carr

Photography by Karen Witynski

Gibbs Smith, Publisher

TO ENRICH AND INSPIRE HUMANKIND

Salt Lake City | Charleston | Santa Fe | Santa Barbara

To my mother, Judith Simpson

First Edition
11 10 09 08 07   5 4 3 2 1

Published by
Gibbs Smith, Publisher
P.O. Box 667
Layton, Utah 84041

Orders: 1.800.835.4993
www.gibbs-smith.com

Designed by CN Design
Printed and bound in China

Library of Congress Cataloging-in-Publication Data

Witynski, Karen, [date]-
  Hacienda courtyards / Karen Witynski and Joe P. Carr ; photographs by Karen Witynski. — 1st ed.
      p. cm.
  ISBN-13: 978-1-4236-0001-5
  ISBN-10: 1-4236-0001-0
  1. Courtyards—Mexico—Influence. 2. Courtyards—Mexico. 3. Haciendas—Mexico—Influence. 4. Haciendas—Mexico. 5. Outdoor living spaces—Mexico—Influence. 6. Outdoor living spaces—Mexico. 7. Gardens—Mexico—Design. 8. Garden structures—Mexico. I. Carr, Joe P., [date]- II. Title.

NA2858.W58 2007
712'.6—dc22
                                                    2006032454

Cover: In Mérida, Yucatán, the courtyard at Casa del Pocito is rich with saturated color and texture.

Back cover: Hacienda Granada's arcaded courtyard features rich color and Mexican handmade bricks.

Half title: A colonial courtyard in Oaxaca, Mexico, features a simple, potted cactus as sculptural art.

Title page: This Oaxaca courtyard highlights the rich textures of old stone, wood, and wrought iron.

Opposite: A unique collection of old stone *metates* create an artful reminder of Oaxaca's traditions.

Following page: In Oaxaca City, colonial architectural traditions blend well with contemporary design.

Contents

Acknowledgments

We are grateful to our friends and colleagues in Mexico, the homeowners, architects, designers, artists, and craftsmen who have shared their knowledge and invited us into their homes.

A heartfelt thanks to the people who helped bring this book to life. First, to my sister Amy Witynski Holmes for her creative inspiration and great editing assistance. We thank our art director, Christine Nasser, for her special design talent and friendship; our agent and friend Betsy Amster, for her expert advice and special support; and the Gibbs Smith team, including editors Madge Baird and Carrie Westover, for their valuable insight and continued dedication to our book series.

We wish to express our most sincere thanks to the many friends and associates who contributed to this book: Architect Salvador Reyes Ríos and designer Josefina Larraín; designers Jim Neeley and David Dow; Jen Lytle of Tierra Yucatan; designer/builder Manolo Vega; architect Alvaro Ponce; Deborah LaChapelle of Casa Santana; Jamie Davis of Portola Paints; and Jim and Nancy Swickard of Hacienda de los Santos in Alamos. Additional thanks to Lynne Wiedman for her expert help with locations in Alamos, Sonora.

We acknowledge with gratitude the assistance of the Yucatán Tourism Office: Carolina Cárdenas Sosa, Secretary of Tourism; Ana Argáez Escalante, Public Relations Director; and Luis Ernesto Villanueva Chac, who lent valuable assistance with our photo shoots.

We are grateful for the assistance of the Sonora Tourism Office: Luis F. Iribe Murrieta, Sergio Cesaretti, Sergio Cota, Adolfo Salido, and Luz del Carmen Parra. A special note of thanks to Javier Guerra Bours for his assistance with our photo shoots.

Additional thanks to the following pioneers who continue to lend valuable support: Roberto Hernández, Claudia Madrazo, Marilu Hernández, Luis Bosoms, Patricia Wohler.

Finally, our deep appreciation to our families for their special support, my mother Judith Simpson, sisters Amy Witynski Holmes, Mara Witynski, Jenny Witynski, brothers-in-law, Marion Holmes and Jeff Schramm. Our gratitude to Joe Carr III, Michael Carr, Jim and Mary Ellen Emery, Verne and Beverly Dwyer for their continued support.

Special thanks to La Misíon de Fray Diego for providing us with wonderful accommodations and impeccable service while on location in Mérida.

We would like to acknowledge Continental Airlines for their support with air transportation during our research trips to Mexico.

Introduction

Hacienda Courtyards was born in the secluded courtyards of Mexico's haciendas and colonial homes, visited while we conducted book research and antiques-buying trips for our design business. Our passion to build and live in a hacienda-style home with a central courtyard germinated in large part from these early design pilgrimages to Mexico. Even though our hacienda courtyard home is rooted in Texas, we delight in the feeling of being in Mexico, thanks to the architectural design, paint colors, and our collection of Mexican antique furniture, old pottery, and once-utilitarian objects that blend together to create our outdoor living room.

Opposite: This Campeche courtyard highlights old stone columns and beamed *portal* ceilings.

For our hacienda design projects in the United States and Mexico, we have repeatedly encountered the lure of indoor-outdoor living and have become enamored with the handcrafted design details that define the centuries-old Mexican courtyard. Our hands-on experience with traditional building and design techniques has inspired us to share our discoveries in this and our previous Mexican design books.

Hidden behind massive walls, the hacienda courtyard is a world unto itself and the heart of every hacienda home. Open to the sky yet enclosed by high walls and graceful stone arcades, the courtyard combines Mexico's rich architectural traditions with flowering gardens and glistening water features, creating a cloistered haven that invites conversation with nature. In traveling from the Yucatán's elegant *henequén* haciendas and colonial homes to the sugar haciendas of Morelos and the silver-mining estates of Alamos, we found the seductions of old colonial courtyards to be many: the time-honored textures of carved stone columns and well-worn pavers; the sight and sound of water splashing from tiled wall fountains into stone vessels; the earthy hues of handmade clay bricks; the visual dance of palm shadows across richly colored stucco walls. No less seducing, a hammock softly swaying beneath a breezy *portal* invited our more relaxed contemplation of the courtyard's gifts.

Previous spread: A peaceful courtyard is framed by graceful arches, Casa Gaber Flores. Opposite: Casa de Sierra Azul's courtyard is rich with carved-stone ornament and a fountain. Above: Plant-filled ceramic pots and carved-stone troughs decorate Casa de Sierra Azul.

13

Alive with these details that conjure the past, today the courtyard is being honed by present-day architects and builders and incorporated as a vital element of hacienda-style home building. Fueled by the heightened interest in restoration and adaptive reuse, the torch of the burgeoning Mexican style movement is being carried by home design professionals who are drawing inspiration from the traditional colors, architectural elements, and natural materials of the Mexican hacienda.

Above: Casa Arroyo Veloz's inviting rooftop garden is alive with color and tropical plants.
Opposite: The colorful courtyard at La Casona de Tita in Oaxaca features lime-based paint.

Through the efforts and innovations of these design professionals, the centuries-old designs and stone techniques of Mexico's masterful craftsmen are being reawakened to spawn contemporary interpretations for renovations and new construction. In the service of authenticity and preserving the sensual appeal of the old elements—be they old beams, entrance gates, flooring, or stone fountains—architects and designers are dedicated to meeting the challenges of customized installations and delays in completion that are often inevitable when obtaining original authentic effects.

Casa de los Artistas blends vibrant color and rich textures. Restored by Salvador Reyes Ríos.

The Mexican courtyard has a complex heritage that blends ancient pre-Hispanic traditions with those of Spanish and Moorish origin. In the sixteenth century, the Spanish Conquest brought European influences to New Spain (Mexico), introducing prominent Spanish architectural styles to the indigenous civilization that was already highly skilled in building. The blend of cultural influences, talented craftsmen, and abundant natural materials combined to produce magnificent architectural treasures. Almost every religious, civil, or domestic building of importance was constructed with one main courtyard or sometimes several courtyards.

Especially inside the austere, massive scale of sixteenth-century convents and government palaces, the courtyard environment provided an aesthetic focus, centered with a stone wellhead or fountain and often surrounded by flowering gardens.

Opposite: The courtyard of this Mexican colonial convent features traditional glazed tiles. Following spread: Hacienda El Alto is rich with traditional stone architectural ornament.

Although courtyards share many common design elements, no two are alike. Generally, they are characterized by towering walls that shelter and protect; flooring of stone, brick, or tile; shady *portales* (covered porches) supported by columns or arcades; water features; and container plants.

Above: Old stone pavers and wood beams grace the *portal* at Hacienda San Antonio Cucul.
Opposite: Elegant Moorish arches surround the colonial courtyard at Villa Maria, Mérida.

The specific design and layout of early hacienda courtyards varied according to the hacienda's geographical region, size, available natural building materials, and the estate's type of production. Serving as both a reception site for horse-drawn carriages and the internal access area to the hacienda's home, stables, offices, and chapel, a hacienda's central courtyard was often a well-used public space. Courtyards for family use were accessed from the living quarters and were designed with generously proportioned *portales* that gave views to that courtyard's garden and fountain. Colonial homes also centered on the refuge of the courtyard, accessed directly from the street through a *záguan* (covered entrance). Depending on the size of the home, there were other smaller courtyards adjacent to kitchens that served as service or washing areas.

Old clay roof tiles and heavy hand-hewn beams bring old-world patina to the covered porches that encircle new courtyards. Ancient recipes for lime-based paint and natural pigments are bringing restored courtyard walls back to life, giving newly constructed walls added depth and richness with their saturated colors and chalky, matte finish. Eighteenth-century column bases adapt to fountain heads, spilling water into new pools. Aquatic gardens are anchored by old stone troughs once used to water hacienda livestock.

Opposite: The chocolate-producing Hacienda La Luz features a lush, tranquil courtyard.

There is an indescribable feeling of peace, tranquility, and protection that one gets from being enveloped in a private yet open-air living space. Over decades of traveling, we have enjoyed many courtyard experiences at friends' Mexican colonial homes. While on hacienda vacations, however, we never imagined how much a secluded courtyard environment could enrich our daily lives. Amidst a full schedule managing design projects and other facets of our business, retreat via our courtyard engages the senses and prompts us to pause and take a breath before walking from one side of the house to the other. We savor the flash of tangerine butterflies or the changing afternoon shadows on the courtyard's yellow ocher walls, made all the more intriguing by protruding stone rainspouts. At night, the tall walls frame a starlit sky, creating a rectangular slice of night that can only be appreciated from within the courtyard. By day, a personal picture screen of continually changing cloud patterns invites unwinding. A staple element of any courtyard, the hammock is a loyal friend, beckoning us to rest for a spell with every gentle breeze.

Opposite: Carved-stone rainspouts, Mexican handmade bricks, roof tiles and antiques adorn Hacienda Granada's arcaded courtyard. Design by Joe P. Carr and Karen Witynski.

Opposite: At Los Dos, an ornate iron gate opens to a lush courtyard and newly added pool.

Above: In Álamos, Hacienda de los Palomas' courtyard features colorful, vine-covered walls.

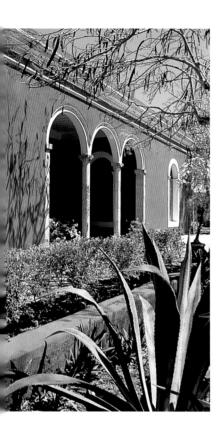

Whether referring to a rural hacienda or colonial home, the term *hacienda* today has become synonymous with a grand, old-world residence. Because Mexico's colonial period saw the construction of both country haciendas and city townhouses simultaneously, these two building types share similar architectural characteristics—including interior courtyard design—which is why both building styles are included in this volume.

Thanks to Mexico's restoration movement in recent years, numerous colonial buildings have been catapulted into the international spotlight. Eighteenth- and nineteenth-century haciendas and city homes have been revived as luxury hotels, restaurants, museums, and cultural centers, thus vacationing homeowners now have access to some of Mexico's most enchanting courtyard spaces. Many of these restored treasures have served as inspiration for travelers who delight in their design details and bring them home to their architects.

Our research for *Hacienda Courtyards* led us to take many detours to off-the-beaten-path locations, including a Tabasco chocolate hacienda hidden in the jungles of Tabasco and the homes and colonial haciendas of the picturesque silver-mining region of Alamos, Sonora, as we felt it was vital to showcase the vast variety of unique courtyard and outdoor living spaces that are serving as inspiration for today's design professionals.

Above: In Mérida, Hacienda Xcumpich features a richly colorful, restored *casa principal*.
Opposite: In the Yucatán, Hacienda Poxila's lush courtyard features an inviting stone lily pond.

Outdoor Living

The hacienda courtyard with its shady *portales* blends water, air, and light, creating a private outdoor living experience. Fountains and inventive water features bring visual refreshment, while furnishings and decorative elements add comfort and personal expression. With the right combination of natural materials and well-placed accents, courtyards, porches, and rooftop terraces become inviting outdoor rooms that allow old and new to converge in a casual, balanced elegance.

Opposite: In the Yucatán, Hacienda Xixim's arcaded *portal* is a heavenly outdoor dining spot.

Designing a house to maximize access and views to the courtyard has become an important priority for hacienda home designers and owners. In Hacienda Granada, our Texas home, the courtyard is an extension of the interior spaces, allowing us to feel connected to the outdoors at all times. Ample windows and six pairs of French doors opening from each of the main rooms give direct access to the courtyard-garden from both wings of the house. The prominence of the courtyard in our home layout is such that no egress can be made from the house except via this central square.

Lending old-world style to long corridors, Mexican colonial benches are a solid choice for courtyard furnishings, as are classic leather sling chairs for comfortable repose. Antique tables, especially those with painted turned-leg bases, add time-worn beauty next to contemporary outdoor chairs. The presence of old stone feeding troughs and conical-shaped water filters—once fixtures in colonial *portales*—is revived in their new roles as planters, contrasting well next to simple terra-cotta pots.

Other elements from the hacienda's utilitarian past also add charm and timelessness to living areas: old stone *metates* once used for grinding spices become displays next to small potted plants. Old corbels once employed to support ceiling beams are now stands for stone planters or supports for wall shelves.

Previous spread: Hacienda Granada features handcrafted roof tiles and Mexican clay bricks.
Opposite: Hacienda Granada's courtyard features an old, bougainvillea-filled *bebedero*.
Above: An old ceramic and Mexican ranch table enliven Hacienda Granada's colorful *zaguan*. Courtyard and zaguan walls feature custom-color lime wash from Portola Paints.

In our own courtyard, pleasing reminders of Mexico's rich history and skilled craftsmen include old coffee *morteros* (mortars), a six-foot-tall wooden cross, a large mesquite vice screw (now sculpture atop an old table), a seven-foot-tall Mayan corn crib carved from a single tree trunk that now holds ferns with the addition of a metal shelf to the inside top, and a fourteen-foot Mexican cypress hacienda *bebedero* (feeding trough) that offers up potted bougainvillea.

Above: Hacienda Granada's *portal* features Mexican antiques and an old carved-stone plaque.

Opposite: An antique Mexican chair and collection of handcarved wooden *manos* decorate the colorful courtyard entrance to Hacienda Granada. Design by Joe P. Carr and Karen Witynski.

Throughout Mexico, courtyard *portal* displays are a unique reflection of the hacienda's productivity, or, in the case of a colonial estate, their collections from bygone days. Outside Mexico City, we've admired portal walls hung with impressive displays of the hacienda's hand-tooled saddles and hats. Prized bull heads are on proud display at haciendas that raise bulls for bullfighting. Nineteenth-century carriages might rest in the shade of *portales* or a handcrafted antique weaving loom. In the Yucatán, ornate iron window grilles pose as art against Mayan blue portal walls, and old hacienda machinery parts such as gears, wheels, and fiber-shredding tools serve as artistic relics of the region's prosperous *henequén* era.

Opposite: Brick accents courtyard walls and entrances at Hacienda La Quintera in Sonora.
Above: An old wooden jail door adds interest to a courtyard wall at Hacienda La Quintera.

41

Most often, access to a hacienda courtyard or colonial patio was through a *záguan* that led directly into the courtyard and was fronted by massive protective doors. Typically of grand-scale width and height, the záguan's doors often featured a smaller door within the main doors, a convenience for individual passage. Both main doors were opened when passage for horses or carriages was required. Once inside the main záguan entrance, a second large gate—made of either wood spindles or decorative iron—allowed the doors to remain open while still securing the property and providing ventilation. Throughout colonial cities, lush courtyards can be glimpsed from open záguan doors beyond these inner gates.

Above: Centuries-old stone pavers line this colonial záguan at La Casona de Tita, Oaxaca.
Opposite: Mexican colonial doors open to reveal Hacienda Granada's záguan and courtyard.

The walls of the solidly hewn courtyard environment were built with adobe, stone, or brick—singly or in combination—and were often plastered and painted. Roofed *portales* surrounding the courtyard were supported by one of several means: round or square wood columns; stone columns crowned by carved capitals; tall masonry arches or plastered brick columns. Providing shade, ventilation, and protection from the elements, the covered porch encompassed the courtyard on two, three, or all four sides, with high walls forming the balance of the enclosure.

Opposite: Casa de los Angelitos' tranquil *portal* features elegant columns and local clay tiles. Above: Mangos drape over a vine-covered wall that is edged in local stone, Alamos, Sonora.

45

The *portal* roof was typically a flat parapet design that varied with the building's architectural style. For this type of roof, the portal ceiling required wooden *vigas* spanned by smaller beams, clay tiles, brick, or wood planks. Carved-stone rainspouts drained water off the roof and into the courtyard. Slanted shed roofs were formed by beams as well, and were often topped with clay roof tiles left exposed on the underside.

A magnificent re-creation of Mexican courtyard life and living has been undertaken by Jim and Nancy Swickard at Hacienda de los Santos, a luxury resort situated in the historic former silver-mining town of Alamos, Sonora. A labor of love for the owners, their impressive restoration story spans fifteen years and includes the revival of four adjacent colonial estates. The properties now commingle on six lush acres and feature six courtyards interconnected through a series of stone walkways, vaulted ceiling tunnels, and footbridges. The lushly landscaped grounds feature four pools, enchanting gardens, and views of the Sierra Madre.

Above: Carved-stone rainspouts extend from a tall parapet roof outlined with brick coping.
Opposite: Courtyard views are plentiful from Hacienda de los Santos' many arcaded *portales*.

The main building's entrance and central courtyard dates from 1700 and originally featured a European-style formal garden. Early explorations revealed that the interior garden-facing walls were originally a series of arches, and that inhabitants lived in rooms open to the courtyard. Over time, the large arches were bricked-in with conventional door and window openings. Another discovery was that the thick walls rested on a heavy, eight-foot-tall stone foundation that continued with adobe in some areas and brick in others. As five of the original columns were still standing, the Swickards replicated their design in the new ones. Today, the grand-scale courtyard space is surrounded by generously proportioned *portales* on three sides, a central swimming pool, and views of the mountains beyond.

Opposite: Hacienda de Los Santos in Alamos, Sonora is resplendent with lush courtyards. Above: This vine-covered courtyard wall features an arched entrance accented with brick. Following spread: Hacienda de Los Santos' grand-scale portales invite outdoor relaxation.

A testament to the couple's love of colonial Mexico's architecture, culture, and decorative arts, Hacienda de los Santos is impressive in its use of traditional elements and colors. The Swickards' use of natural materials for reconstruction includes more than 45,000 square feet of hand-cut stone tiles. Several original stone *canales* (rainspouts) were found intact and were replicated for the spacious courtyard. Remnants of beautifully colored plaster found during the restoration inspired Nancy's selection of the hacienda's color scheme. Moreover, not a single 2 x 4 inhabits the nearly 90,000 square feet of the hacienda, and the Swickards' guests are quickly enamored by that fact. Outdoor stone and brick fireplaces and a plethora of carved-stone elements enhance the atmosphere of authenticity at Hacienda de los Santos. The namesake of the resort, a vast collection of antique *santos*, as well as *retablos* and other antiques, spills from the Swickards' interiors into the courtyards and gives beautiful unity to the artful spaces.

Above: In Alamos, Sonora, Hacienda de los Santos features myriad *portales* for outdoor living.
Opposite: The use of locally-crafted materials is prevalent at Hacienda de los Santos, Alamos.
Following spread: In Alamos, La Querencia's courtyard features an impressive cactus garden.

Above: An old stone water vessel adds interesting textures to a colorful brick courtyard.

Opposite: Ceramic wall planters add interest to the wall fountain at Los Dos, Mérida.

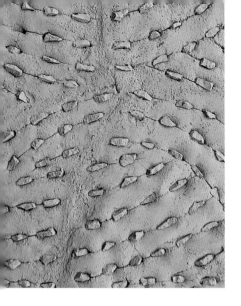  

Courtyard Textures

The rich, time-honored textures of stone, earth, wood, and tile lend depth and distinction to courtyard spaces, proudly revealing old-world character marks and age. From lime-based paint and hand-chiseled stone pavers to unique stucco techniques and hand-hewn beams that support clay tile porch roofs, the outdoor architecture of Mexico's courtyards is characterized by a distinct vocabulary of design materials and textures dictated by geographical location and available natural resources.

Opposite: Oaxaca's natural green stone adds color and rich texture to this arcaded courtyard.

Our earliest encounters with Mexico's alluring courtyard elements were had while on antiques—buying trips for our gallery. Throughout Mexico, we were privileged to view old treasures and colonial furniture in a variety of settings. The remote warehouses and open-air storage spaces we discovered were part of old haciendas or colonial homes either under restoration or uninhabited, providing ample space for the cleaning and repairing of the dozens of massive doors and myriad objects stacked within.

Above: Newly carved stone and natural, rustic stone planters create an intriguing juxtaposition.
Opposite: An old colonial stone wellhead has been adapted to a fountain at Hacienda El Alto.

While traipsing over piles of old beams, sorting through doors stacked against walls and deciphering a puzzle of cut-stone ornaments strewn over the cobbled floor, we could not help but be drawn into the incredible details of the surrounding courtyard environment. While measuring old wooden tables and trunks, our attention wandered to the rough-hewn stone pavers underfoot. Our camera was soon focused on the elements beneath, above, and beyond the stacked and strewn antiques that were the original intention for our visit. The beauty of golden-hued stones, weathered window grilles, mottled oxblood red walls and the worn patina of the ornate wrought-iron entrance gate intrigued us. In following a blooming vine's winding stretch from the ground, up over a pile of ox yokes and nail-studded gates, to finally encircle a carved serpent rainspout, we were unwittingly captured by the lures of courtyard life.

It was while photographing the beauty of courtyard life that we began asking questions about the variations in materials and pigments used for the lime-based paint that were fundamental to the texture and colors on courtyard walls.

Opposite, clockwise: In the Yucatán, small chinked stones in stucco walls create mesmerizing patterns and a bold design statement; old courtyard walls constructed with both stone and brick create a unique blend of surface textures when left exposed; *portal* ceilings in Alamos, Sonora are rich with textural design, thanks to hand-adzed wood beams and natural materials; Oaxaca's natural green stone creates an interesting graphic when aligned in rows in a large space.

Our subsequent travels for our seven books allowed us to crisscross the country and discover a variety of courtyard textures and designs. In Michoacán, we visited an early colonial estate that featured original stone flooring under the courtyard's covered *portales*. We marveled at the unique texture that has filled spaces between stone pavers for centuries—animal vertebrae. In the mountains of Jalisco, an adobe hacienda's courtyard made innovative use of original stone watering troughs that flaunted rich textures while spilling over with blooming flowers. In the pulque-producing region of Hidalgo, a turreted castle-style hacienda featured in its inviting garden courtyard deep *portales* richly painted with green wainscots that were accented with colonial-patterned blue and green stencils. In Campeche, we relaxed in a colonial courtyard surrounded by ornate Moorish arches that lent the space a grand sophistication.

Above: A dramatic colonial stone arch creates a rich backdrop to this Michoacán courtyard.
Opposite: The weathered textures of colonial stone are witness to Hacienda Uayamón's past.

Stone

In addition to use in functional architectural elements such as door and window surrounds, cornices, columns, and capitals, stone is shaped into fountains, table bases, vessels for plants, and a variety of sacred and decorative accents, including crosses and saints.

Throughout Mexico, the principal colors of stone used for residential building are variations on volcanic grey, gold, and rose. Fashioned for square floor tiles in a variety of finishes from rough to smooth, colors vary with region and origin. In Oaxaca, the natural green stone found there is used for flooring and myriad architectural details.

Above and opposite: This Oaxaca courtyard highlights the beauty of handcarved local stone.

In the Yucatán, thick limestone pavers are hand-chiseled to replicate the uneven surface effect of old stones, and are used for outdoor patios. Conchuela stone, which features a fossilized texture, is popular for *nicho* surrounds, tiles, and decorative accents such as fountain spouts. A unique favorite found outside of Mexico City is a stone called *madera* (wood). Resembling the look of wood grain, madera stone appears in cream, gold, and brown tones.

Hand-chiseled stone pavers add old-world textures to the Casa Reyes-Larraín courtyard. Restoration and design by architect Salvador Reyes Ríos and designer Josefina Larraín.

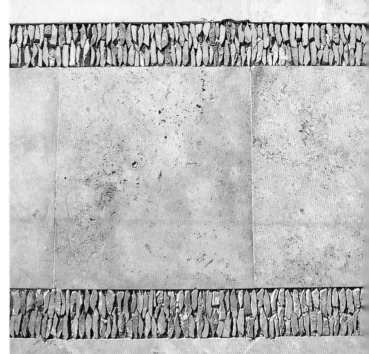

The pre-Hispanic tradition of *rajueleado* is a stone-chinking method used in exterior walls that features a repetition of small stones chinked from larger ones, placed by hand to punctuate stuccoed walls. Mesmerizing effects are produced from this old technique, both when the surface is completely chinked and when more open design patterns are made with the creative placement of stones. Most commonly seen in white limestone, rajueleado is also dramatic when the natural, orange-hued Ticul stone is used. Behind a waterfall fountain, the rough chinked-stone texture offers sharp contrast to the fluidity of water. Decorative bands of chinked stones can also embellish floors, creating bold outlines or accents upon stone tile or colored concrete surfaces.

Opposite: A stone-chinked (rajueleado) wall offers a dramatic backdrop to a tiled outdoor bathtub at Merimo Nah. Designed by architect Salvador Reyes Ríos and Josefina Larrain.

From beams and carved corbels to doors and columns, the timeless beauty of wood brings weathered warmth to courtyard spaces adorned in stone and brick. Square or round *vigas* (beams) are paired with wooden corbels on *portal* ceilings for a traditional look. For the doors and gates, hand-adzed wood planks were reinforced with handwrought braces and *clavos* (large nail heads). Hacienda entrance doors, built with defensive measures in mind, radiate strength and a captivating sense of history. Today, antique doors and spindled gates—natural or with layers of old paint—serve as ideal courtyard entrances and strike a grand impression upon approach.

Opposite: The portal at Hacienda Los Laureles in Oaxaca features wood beams and clay tiles.
Above: Wood beams, corbels, and doors add warmth to a variety of outdoor courtyard spaces.

Clay Tile and Bricks

Clay and its infinite color variations produce a wide variety of clay tiles and bricks in Mexico. In regions with plentiful clay earth, high-fired bricks have long been favored for wall, column, and ceiling construction, including *bóvedas* (vaulted ceilings), as well as flooring under covered porches. Clay bricks and tiles crafted in one region produce traditional red tones, while others are a soft light brown or golden yellow. In specific regions where manganese deposits are found, the mineral is added to clay floor tiles to naturally darken red clay tiles to a beautiful chocolate brown. Handmade barrel-shaped clay roof tiles also offer rich color variations and weather into alluring textures. In addition to covering courtyard porches, these tiles are also seen atop stuccoed garden walls, offering protection. When brick or clay tile is chosen for beneath covered porches, stone is often used to transition from the edge of the *portal* before the exposed stone courtyard begins.

Above: In Alamos, Hacienda La Colorada's old stable arches have become garden ornament.
Opposite: The beauty of the local clay brick is found throughout Hacienda La Colorada, Alamos.

Above left: Clay roof tiles protect elegant windows and doors at Hacienda X'canatun, Mérida.

Above: Richly textural roof tile is a highlight of this spacious courtyard in Mérida, Yucatán.

Opposite: In the Yucatán, Hotel Marioneta's owners creatively accommodated a dramatically tall palm tree when building a red clay tiled porch roof to their courtyard's covered portal.

For centuries, glazed Talavera tiles have been favored to decorate
fountains, stair risers, or wall wainscots. In Puebla, the state known for
its rich Talavera tile traditions, building facades, *záguans*, and courtyards
feature colorful hand-painted tiles in impressive combinations with
unglazed tiles. A favorite old convent features tiled fountains surrounded
by gardens and two-story arcades covered in Talavera tile—a mesmerizing
geometric design of hand-painted patterned tiles with unglazed clay tiles.

Above: Talavera tile adds decorative interest to this winding stairway and old colonial home.
Opposite: This colonial courtyard in Puebla features mesmerizing walls of old Talavera tile.

80

Mexico's vibrant color heritage plays an important role in courtyard spaces. As haciendas and colonial homes were predominately constructed with stone, walls were finished with a lime-based stucco and lime-based paint called *cal*, mixtures that shared the quality of porosity compatible with a stone surface. Traditional colors, obtained from earthen pigments, included oxblood red and yellow ocher. Lime's porosity encourages stone walls to breathe, allowing moisture to escape without damaging the wall's painted surface. The effect of cal is a soft, matte finish that conjures old-world courtyard walls.

Today, designers in the United States are using lime-based paint for courtyard walls as well as interior spaces, in response to homeowners' desires to replicate the texture and finish of the old walls encountered on their travels. California-based Portola Paints & Glazes, named after the Spanish explorer Gaspar de Portola, is one of today's innovative paint leaders bringing old lime-based paint recipes to today's design projects. Portola's locally made lime paints are reproduced on handmade color cards using actual product and colors, giving clients a true sample that excels any printed approximation of color. Portola offers custom color matching as well as a palette of rich colors ranging from papaya to Spanish lavender.

Opposite: Traditional lime paint brings a rich weathered feel to Casa del Pocito's fountain.

Specialty finisher Bob Quinn has used Portola's lime paint on a number of wall surfaces: raw stucco and plaster, concrete, and previously painted walls. As the paint's lime "blooms," or rises to the surface at differing levels, the result is a slightly mottled look that echoes the weathered look of old walls. Quinn's method is to apply the paint with a large brush and random strokes. The process of misting the walls while the paint is drying, or soon thereafter, enhances the lime blooming process and increases the variation in lightness and darkness of shades. His clients' preferences have been for saturated earthy tones: oranges, browns, terra-cottas, yellows, and golds.

Opposite and above: Alive with the rich textures of local stone, carved wood, and traditional lime-based paint, La Casona de Tita's Oaxaca courtyard offers guests beauty and tranquility.

Aquatic Gardens

The sight and sound of *agua (water)*, whether spilling from a Talavera-tiled central fountain or trickling down a stone aqueduct fed by a hacienda water tank-turned-pool, has a pleasing effect to courtyard living.

Drawing inspiration from Mexico's old stone elements and traditional water systems—both underground and aboveground—architects, builders, and homeowners are exploring adaptive reuse of the elements that old haciendas employed to efficiently collect, store, and distribute water. In the Yucatán, these integral elements included cisterns, storage tanks, aqueduct channels, waterspouts, and *bebederos* (watering troughs).

Opposite: At Merimo Nah in Mérida, an aquatic garden features an old stone column base.

Aquatic gardens beautifully envelop the raised swimming pool at Merimo Dah in the Yucatán.
Home restoration and design by architect Salvador Reyes Ríos and designer Josefina Larraín.

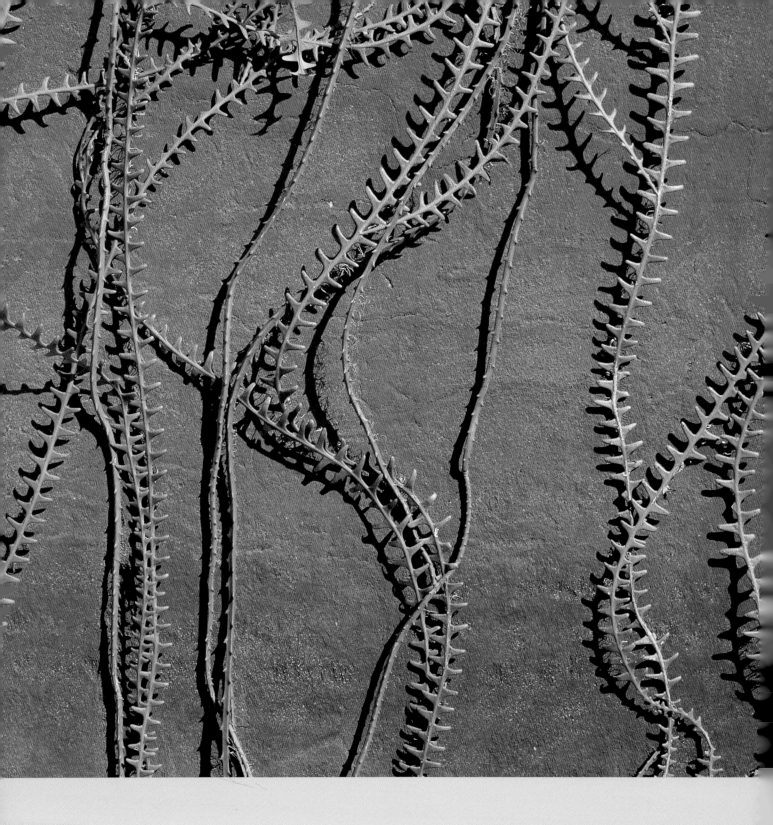

Above: A tropical vine in Oaxaca climbs a colorful wall creating a mesmerizing statement.

Opposite: Once part of an old aqueduct system, this stone has become a unique water spout.

Old stone radiates permanence and brings a textural palette to water features. Once used to remove rainwater from hacienda roofs, hand-carved *canales* are newly fashioned into walls to feed aquatic gardens. Stone feeding troughs removed from crumbling corrals now sit on pool corners; old column capitals, adapted with newly cut channels, stand as fountainheads trickling water into new pools. At Hacienda Cucul and Hacienda Ochil, as well as many other colonial estates, long stone *bebederos,* formerly used to water horses and livestock, boast colorful water hyacinths and lily pads.

Opposite: A stone fountain spills water into the koi pond at Casa de los Angelitos, Alamos.
Above: Bamboo and tall trees surround this carved-stone fountain at Hacienda Xcumpich.

93

Many of Mexico's colonial water fountains had round or octagonal bases and were crafted in hearty proportions from carved stone. In small courtyards, wall fountains were favored and featured stone backsplashes and a semicircular base, rounded along the top edge. Stone wellheads, once the centerpiece of a hacienda's or colonial home's courtyard, are being retooled to become elegantly simple fountains, retaining the old stone base design.

Previous spread: Casa de los Angelitos' tropical courtyard is alive with the sound of water.
Opposite: In Alamos, La Querencia's wall fountain features clay tiles and a carved-stone frame.
Above: A traditional colonial-style fountain base is paired with a tiled and stone wall spout.

Above and opposite: Hacienda Santa Cruz's casa de máquina features a tranquil fountain.

At Casa Santana, a wall stone fountain in the tropical backyard draws inspiration from owner Deborah LaChapelle's penchant for old *bebederos* at her favorite Yucatán haciendas. Taking advantage of an existing hole in a shaded stone garden wall and the property's water well, LaChapelle secured three old hacienda *canales* at varying heights to spill water to feed a rectangular stone basin. Incorporating stone and organic elements into the restored colonial home turned bed-and-breakfast in Mérida gives her design a natural grotto feeling.

Opposite: An inviting wall fountain at Casa Santana features old hacienda stone rainspouts. Above: A stone aqueduct channels water throughout Cibolo Creek Ranch's central courtyard.

Success with the stone fountain led LaChapelle to design another fountain fed from Casa Santana's swimming pool. Spotting a *pila* (stone basin) with a broken corner at a local antiques yard, LaChapelle envisioned water trickling out the open edge and into the pool. Once she set the pila on the pool corner and set up the channeling system, she realized the flow of water was too rapid. The addition of stone spheres provided enough diversion for the water to slow it to her desired tranquil trickle.

Above: At Casa Santana, water trickles from an antique stone trough into the swimming pool.
Opposite: In Alamos, Sonora, the spacious courtyard at La Quinta features a large fountain.

An old sugar hacienda in Morelos features a favorite wall fountain emerging from a stone basin against a colorfully stuccoed wall. Beautifully curved strips of stone surround the carved fountainhead and appear from afar to be dynamically curled pieces sculpted from the stucco. Other favorite fountains are in the state of Puebla, where numerous government buildings, convents, colonial homes, and haciendas pay homage to the city's colorful history of glazed Talavera tile via backsplashes and fountain bases covered in beautiful hand-painted patterns.

Opposite: Tropical plants surround this reflecting pool, Hacienda San Gabriel de las Palmas. Above: Decorative carved stone accents a wall fountain at Hacienda de Cortes, Cuernavaca.

Stone spheres punctuate a dramatic courtyard water feature at Hacienda El Alto in Morelia.

Above: In the Yucatán, Hacienda San Antonio Cucul features an arcaded, old stone aqueduct.

Opposite: At Merimo Nah, an aquatic garden pleases with the soft sound of trickling water.

108

Opposite: At Hacienda Sodzil, lush plantings envelop the tranquil lily pond. Mérida, Yucatán.

Above: A colonial bench is a welcome addition to this garden courtyard. Joe P. Carr Design.

Swimming Spaces

In the Yucatán and elsewhere, Mexico's centuries-old water heritage is being redefined in the contemporary design of pool gardens and water spaces. Siting swimming pools amid traditional or unusual architectural elements has become increasingly prevalent in recent years. Many projects center swimming spaces around old columns, beneath or next to arcaded facades, or even "inside" old seventeenth-century rooms that open to roofless spaces, as seen at Hacienda Puerta Campeche in the state of Campeche. The dramatic use of classic architecture is reminiscent of ancient Rome and yet is distinctly fresh with Mexican influences.

Opposite: Old stone columns dominate the dramatic pool at Hacienda Cortes in Cuernavaca.

At Hacienda Uayamón in Campeche, we delighted in swimming around centuries-old tall stone columns formerly supporting an uncompleted ice factory. The pool remains one of our favorites due to the awe-inspiring architectural juxtaposition and the peaceful seclusion of stone walls that have become one with tree roots. Old, elegant building columns are also center stage in the inviting pool at Hacienda Cortes in Cuernavaca.

At Los Dos, a restored colonial-style home in Mérida, owners David Sterling and Keith Heitke found inspiration for their backyard swimming space in the Yucatán's grand arcaded hacienda *portales*. To combine a three-meter-deep portal and swimming pool into their relatively small backyard, they sited one end of the pool slightly beneath the portal so as not to overwhelm the entire yard/garden space. Accessed by several wide steps, the pool features a row of stone columns submerged in water, bringing an element of soulful antiquity literally inside the pool.

Opposite: At Los Dos, elegant arches appear to float across the courtyard garden and pool. Above: In the Yucatán, Los Dos' tropical courtyard features wall-embedded hammock hooks.

A most impressive example of water accompanied by old architecture can be seen at Hacienda Puerta Campeche, a luxury hotel in the historic heart of Campeche, a UNESCO World Heritage Site. A series of elegant seventeenth-century houses, this estate was artfully restored by Grupo Plan under the direction of architect Luis Bosoms. While inside the cool, shadowy presence of ancient stone walls, one can float through a series of pool "rooms" that connect through tall open doorways then out into sun-filled, roofless rooms that open onto tropical gardens.

Above: Hacienda Puerta Campeche features a series of beautifully restored colonial homes.
Opposite: A white hammock skims the water's sparkling surface at Hacienda Puerta Campeche.

Grand-style hacienda stone columns also support the *portal* at Casa Colonial, a restored 1840s home-turned-boutique hotel. The ninety-foot portal stretches between the old house in front and owners Philippe and Dominique Duneton's new two-story guest wing. Visible from both old and new parts of the house, as well as the centerpiece of the backyard, their rectangular pool creates a peaceful haven enhanced by hammocks and deep sofas. Views to the pool are framed by elegant white curtains that billow in the tropical breezes and protect guests from afternoon sun. The lime-based painted facade is a pleasing backdrop to the pool in *rojo hacienda*, or hacienda red, outlined by white arches.

Above and opposite: Merimo Nah's courtyard features a raised pool and water gardens, Mérida.

Opposite: A grotto-style fountain flows into the pool at The Bishop's House, Alamos, Sonora.
Above: Bougainvillea spills over the courtyard wall to beautifully frame a stone birdbath.
Following spread: An inviting hammock floats over the water at Casa Barrera in the Yucatán.

At Casa Aurora, a hacienda-inspired home in Mérida, builder-designer Manolo Vega created a peaceful haven that celebrates outdoor living, the soothing sights and sounds of water, and Yucatán's traditional materials, textures, and colors.

Grand-scale proportions and thick zapote beams support an eighteen-foot ceiling that gives a robust, old-world aesthetic to the hacienda's open, cool-tiled living room and dining hall. The two rooms extend ninety feet and provide open views of the grand-scale pool, adjoining a thatched-roof palapa, water gardens, and palm-lined garden.

As Manolo Vega and wife Aurora have always felt a special connection to the ocean, they wanted to create the continuous breezes and infinite views the shoreline provides, feeling protected within the solidity of a hacienda-type structure. The pier that leads from the master bedroom to the swimming pool, inspired by the old wooden pier at the Yucatán port of Chicxulub, extends the beach aesthetic and further connects the interior spaces with the outdoors. A boundary wall in full view of the living hall posed a particular challenge to Vega's desire to honor the views of the ocean. He solved the problem by painting the wall blue to simulate the sky. Clearly a successful solution, now the wall disappears into the sky and the pool appears to be visually framed only by the tall line of palms.

Opposite: Casa Aurora surrounds a spacious central courtyard featuring a palm-lined garden, thatched-roof palapa, and pier leading to the pool. Designed by Manolo Vega, Mérida, Yucatán.

Above: Casa Aurora's palm-lined courtyard features rich stone textures and aquatic gardens.

Above: Casa Aurora's wooden pier creates a unique and inviting approach to the swimming pool.

Resources

We invite you to visit our gallery, **Joe P. Carr Design**, for Mexican colonial antiques and hacienda style elements, including old doors, wrought-iron window grilles, ceiling beams and flooring. In addition to colonial trunks, benches, tables, chairs and armoires, we also offer an exclusive line of iron lockplate sconces, lanterns and chandeliers. Our hacienda doors are hand-crafted in Mexico and are available in custom sizes. Decorative accents include antique ceramics, rare Mexican textiles, culinary antiques and old stone elements. Design services available.

Please visit our website for Mexican design news:

www.mexicanstyle.com

AUTHORS' MAILING ADDRESS:

JOE P. CARR/KAREN WITYNSKI
3267 Bee Caves Rd. #107-181
Austin, TX 78746
512 370-9663
512 327-8284
www.mexicanstyle.com

Authors' Gallery:
JOE P. CARR DESIGN
3601 Bee Caves Road
at Barton Springs Nursery
Austin, TX 78746
512 370-9663
512 327-8284

KAREN WITYNSKI
Architectural &
Interior Photography
512 370-9663
512 327-8284

This page, top: Authors Joe P. Carr and Karen Witynski. Above left: Traditional Yucatán door with grilled shutters. Above: Colonial bench, painted doors and handcarved coffee mortar.

Opposite: Colonial doors, old Mexican furniture and accents, Joe P. Carr Design.

ARCHITECTS / BUILDERS

REYES RIOS + LARRAIN
Restoration, Architecture,
Design & Landscape
Salvador Reyes Ríos
Josefina Larraín Lagos
Mérida, Yucatán
999 923-5808
reyesrios@prodigy.net.mx

PLAN ARQUITECTOS
Luis Bosoms, Architect
Mexico City, Mexico
555 257-0097
www.grupoplan.com

ALVARO PONCE
Architect
Mérida, Yucatán
999 943-3075
corvina@tponce.com

HENRY PONCE, Architect
Mérida, Yucatán
999 926-0018
999 947-2233
www.henryponce.com

MANOLO VEGA
Builder/Designer
Mérida, Yucatán
999 970-1298
mvega62@prodigy.net.mx

DANIEL LOPEZ SALGADO
Architect
Oaxaca, Oaxaca
951 132-4290

HERNAN PIMENTEL, Architect
Pátzcuaro, Michoacán
434 342-1098

DESIGNERS

SALVADOR REYES RIOS
JOSEFINA LARRAIN
Mérida, Yucatán
999 923-5808
jlarrain@sureste.com

WISECRACKER DESIGN
Jim Neeley + David Dow
jimneeley@aol.com

JOE P. CARR DESIGN
Joe P. Carr/Karen Witynski
Austin, Texas &
Mérida, Yucatán
512 327-8284
www.mexicanstyle.com

Left: Mexican Hacienda door available through Joe P. Carr Design, Austin.

Above: Carved stone rainspouts, Hacienda de los Santos, Alamos.

Opposite, clockwise from top left: Hacienda Santa Rosa, Yucatán; Posada La Basilica, Pátzcuaro; a colorful hacienda entrance features lime paint, Portola Paints.

RESOURCES

MOSAICOS TRAQUI
Floor Tile, Yucatán
988 916-1500
traqui84@prodigy.net.mx

MOSAICOS LA PENINSULAR
Floor Tile, Yucatán
999 923-1196
www.paginasprodigy.com/
mosaicospeninsular

PORTOLA PAINTS
Studio City, CA
818 623-9053
www.portolapaints.com

QUINN INTERIORS
Specialty Paint Finishes
Los Angeles, CA
818 517-6155
www.quinninteriors.biz

REVIVALS DESIGNS
Design & Specialty Paint
Finishes
Corinne Enslin
Los Angeles, CA
818 509-9123
revivalsdesign@sbcglobal.net

The Yucatán's colonial charms include the city of Izamal (below), Hacienda Santa Rosa (right) and Hacienda San Antonio Cucul (bottom).

Travel Guide

Mexico's captivating colonial cities are an attractive destination offering visitors architectural splendor amidst elegant eighteenth-century hotels and restored hacienda resorts. Continental Airlines flies to thirty Mexico destinations—including key colonial cities—more than any other U.S. carrier. Continental also offers more flights from the U.S. to Mexico than any other carrier.

U.S. Reservations (800) 231-0856
Mexico Reservations 01 (800) 900-5000
www.continental.com

Continental Airlines

HOTELS

**HACIENDA DE LOS SANTOS
RESORT & SPA**
Alamos, Sonora
647 428-0222
www.haciendadelossantos.com

HOTEL COLONIAL
Alamos, Sonora
647 428-1371
www.alamoshotelcolonial.com

CASA DE LOS TESOROS
Alamos, Sonora
647 428-0010

LA QUINTA LUNA
Cholula, Puebla
222 247-8915
www.laquintaluna.com

HACIENDA LOS LAURELES
Oaxaca, Oaxaca
951 501-5300
www.hotelhaciendaloslaureles.com

CASA DE SIERRA AZUL
Oaxaca, Oaxaca
951 514-7171
www.mexonline.com/sierrazul.htm

LA CASONA DE TITA
Oaxaca, Oaxaca
951 516-1402
www.hotellacasonadetitaoaxaca.com.mx

HOTEL POSADA LA BASILICA
Pátzcuaro, Michoacán
434 342-1108
www.posadalabasilica.com

HACIENDA TEYA
Hotel—Restaurant
Mérida, Yucatán
999 988-0801

**THE HACIENDAS
THE LUXURY COLLECTION
OWNERS: GRUPO PLAN**
Managed by: Starwood
Hotels & Resorts
800 325-3589 in the U.S.
999 923-8089 in Mexico
www.luxurycollection.com
Hacienda San José Cholul, Yucatán
Hacienda Santa Rosa, Yucatán
Hacienda Temozón, Yucatán
Hacienda Uayamón, Campeche
Hacienda Puerta Campeche

HACIENDA XCANATUN
Mérida, Yucatán
999 941-0213
www.xcanatun.com

HOTEL MARIONETAS
Mérida, Yucatán
999 928-3377
www.hotelmarionetas.com

LA MISION DE FRAY DIEGO
Mérida, Yucatán
999 924-1111
www.lamisiondefraydiego.com

VILLA MARIA
Mérida, Yucatán
999 923-3357
www.villamariamerida.com

CASA SANTANA
Mérida, Yucatán
999 923-3331
www.casasantana.com

HACIENDA SANTA CRUZ
South of Mérida, Yucatán
999 910-4549
www.haciendasantacruz.com

**LOS DOS GUESTHOUSE
& COOKING SCHOOL**
Mérida, Yucatán
999 928-1116
www.los-dos.com

Above: La Misión de Fray Diego hotel features an elegant portal.

141

YUCATAN

YUCATAN TOURISM
Mérida, Yucatán
999 930-3760
www.mayayucatan.com
www.yucatan.gob.mx

**FUNDACION HACIENDAS
EN EL MUNDO MAYA**
Mérida, Yucatán
999 928-7750
www.haciendasmundomaya.com

**TIERRA YUCATAN
REAL ESTATE**
Mérida, Yucatán
999 923-7615
999 930-9684
www.tierra-maya.com

**YUCATAN TODAY
TOURIST GUIDE**
Mérida, Yucatán
999 927-8531
www.yucatantoday.com

SONORA

SONORA TOURISM
662 217-0060
www.visitasonora.com
www.gotosonora.com

ALAMOS HOME TOURS
Alamos, Sonora
647 428-0614
lynne8877@msn.com

ALAMOS REALTY
647 428-0350
www.alamosrealty.com

AMIGOS DE EDUCACION DE ALAMOS
APDO Postal 123
Alamos, Sonora 85763
647 428-0614
*Non-profit organization
that raises funds to award
scholarships and assistance to
children who otherwise would be
unable to receive an education
beyond the sixth grade.*

DESIGN CREDITS

Casa Aurora: Manolo Vega
Casa Colonial: Philipe and Dominique Duneton
Casa del Pocito: Jim Neeley and David Dow
Casas Reyes-Larraín: Salvador Reyes Ríos & Josefina Larraín
Casa Santana: Deborah LaChapelle
Hacienda El Alto: Ed Holler and Sam Saunders
Hacienda Granada: Joe P. Carr and Karen Witynski
Hacienda Santa Cruz: Fiona St. Clair
Hotel Marionetas: Daniel and Sofi Bosco
La Casona de Tita: Daniel Lopez Salgado, Architect
La Querencia: Tom and Twyla Harkness
Los Dos: David Sterling and Keith Heitke
Merimo Nah: Salvador Reyes Ríos & Josefina Larraín
Residence Page 78, Alvaro Ponce, Architect
Residence Pages 122–123, Peter Law and Bob Tate

Above: Hacienda Itzincab Camara

Opposite: Authors Karen Witynski and Joe P. Carr in Mexico with friends Rene and Juan.

MEXICAN DESIGN BOOK SERIES
by KAREN WITYNSKI & JOE P. CARR